TRANSHUMANISM
What is it?

NATASHA VITA-MORE

CONTENTS

INTRODUCTION

Over the past three decades, I have encountered vast, complex, and consuming assumptions about the transhuman and transhumanism. Interactions at conferences, university lectures, cafes across the planet, people have asked me what it is. It is not a mystery, nor should it be. Consider what has occurred in the beginning of the past three decades—the Advanced Research Projects Agency Network (ARPANET) switches its technology to TCP/IP, marking the moment of the "Internet", which lead to the World Wide Web. Michael Jackson produced the signature "moonwalk" dance on TV's special "Motown 25: yesterday, Today, Forever". The Hubble Space Telescope was launched into orbit in 1990 and in 2005, the Cassini-Huygens made a soft landing on Titan.

The Technology Era provided hopes and challenges, but most of society remained the same. People continued to worry about money, jobs, families, disease, and loss. While medical science has uncovered cures for many diseases, cancer continues to be on the rise, as death rates have increased since the mid-1980s. Nevertheless, surprising new cures are continually uncovered. We are now in the Life Extension Era.

Transhumanism's time has arrived. It has struck a cord with many who want to fight the onslaught of disease and live longer healthy lives. It is no longer a complex concept that encounters vast and often confusing questions. The earlies ideas, terms, and themes transhumanists have been writing and talking about for three decades have become mainstream. Nevertheless, there are still some unanswered questions and there are misconceptions that pop up here and there, largely because of cut and paste accountings of what was thought of as true some ten, twenty or thirty years ago. The book aims to help to clarify some of these misconceptions. Too often small talk takes precedence over academic rigor, or journalistic hype takes priority over what really happened. There are many issues that are frightening to people about the future. There is no fault in this, the future can be daunting. Yet, once the transhumanist ideas are explored and understood they start becoming second nature. So, there is no worry about any awkwardness in reading this book for those of you who are new to transhumanism. I was once awkward too, and then it became second nature. The more you engage in the unknowns, the more you adapt to change, the more you challenge your own thinking, the more alive and excited you will become about being part of this Transhumanist Era of life extension.

Reflection

I have been asked why I became involved with transhumanism at a time when I could have made other choices based on prodigious opportunities. Yet, those choices would not have made me happy.

My passion is in support of healthier, more durable, and longer lasting bodies and for a more humane humanity. This passion stems from experience with disease and injury and the struggle to overcome these obstacles. I have witnessed the misfortunes of others whose disease and injuries were debilitating to the point beyond what one could reasonably imagine. Many years ago, I volunteered for the Home for Incurables, a facility where people were so malformed that they were not allowed in public. I also volunteered at various hospitals, and with friends, adopted families during Holiday seasons and delivered food and gifts to those who had less than us. While in college, I watched my father volunteer for St. Jude's Children's Hospital where I observed him sketch children with incurable cancers and awaiting a cure.

When my beloved brother suffered from illness and passed away from deep, unresolved sadness, I knew that cognitive fragility must be overcome. My darling mother, who lived into her 100th year although plagued with dementia toward the end, did not lose the glimmer in her eyes nor did I relinquish my desire to see aging overcome.

> "The fact that the maximum human lifespan is limited to a little more than a single century, most of which is spent resisting disease, has compelled a small yet growing community of individuals, including the author, to take up the challenges … exploring the domain of life extension and carrying an unfaltering interest about future possibilities of protecting and sustaining life in biological and nonbiological systems.

> "Because biotechnology, nanomedicine, robotics, artificial intelligence and virtual environments are now upon us along with realistic possibilities for engineering genetics to intervene with the damage caused by cellular mutations and aging, to repair the biological body, and to build new bodies, there is reason to be more enthused than ever to explore how these emerging and speculative technologies fit into the … humanities. Thus, this dissertation sets out to investigate the potential emerging and speculative media for life expansion, the locus in which this study is located" (Vita-More, 2012, p. 14).

The question is what will we become? This book begins to answer that question.

VALUE ELEMENTS	TRANSHUMANIST THINKING	TRADITIONAL SOCIO-POLITICAL STANCE
ADVOCATES HUMAN LIFE SUSTAINABLE	10	0
ADVOCATES REMAINING BIOLOGICAL	2	10
BIOTECHNOLOGICAL MEDIATION ASSEPTABLE	10	5
OPPOSES GENETIC ENGINEERING	0	10
EMPATHY AND HUMANNESS CRUCIAL	10	9
SUPPORTS RIGHT TO DIE	10	2
LBGT IS A NEW NORMAL	10	5
ADVOCATES TAX TRANSPARENCY	10	4
ALL GOVERNANCE REQURIED CONTINUING EDUCATION	10	2

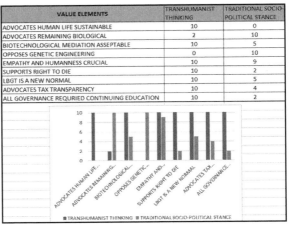

CHAPTER 1

TRANSHUMANISM, WHAT IS IT?

Transhumanism is a philosophy, a worldview and a movement.

To explain the philosophy of transhumanism is not only daring, it can be daunting. From the philosophical worldview to the ever-growing movement, differing transhumanist perspectives have taken shape. Nevertheless, the core ideas and central themes, purpose and goals, that give transhumanism its fundamental identity have not changed and continue to be its most valued assets.

Philosophy

Transhumanism is an intellectual and cultural movement that supports the ethical use of technology and evidence-based science to improve the human condition.

Max More defined modern transhumanism in 1990 as "Philosophies of life (such as extropian perspectives) that seek the continuation and acceleration of the evolution of intelligent life beyond its currently human form and human limitations by means of science and technology, guided by life-promoting principles and values. With further explanation, More writes:

"What is the core content of this philosophy? A simple yet helpful way to grasp its nature is to think of transhumanism as 'trans-humanism' plus 'transhuman-ism'. 'Trans-humanism' emphasizes the philosophy's roots in Enlightenment humanism. From here comes the emphasis on progress (its possibility and desirability, not its inevitability), on taking personal charge of creating better futures rather than hoping or praying for them to be brought about by supernatural forces, on reason, technology, scientific method, and human creativity rather than faith" (More, 2013).

Worldview

Rapid growth curves have triggered questions about a shifting human paradigm that still remain unanswered by countless theories, strategies, and religious views. Yet, transhumanists have been answering many of these questions for decades. Despite varied backgrounds, the focus has always been on the use of ethical technology to improve human circumstances and to openly address and debate unexpected challenges of technology in relation to what the future human might become. Transhumanism it is not located in any one field or enterprise. Its scope is continually evolving on par with the social, scientific, economic, political and technological landscapes. As a dynamic, adaptive system that engages numerous points of view, transhumanism is needed today more than ever.

Throughout the world people are undergoing unhealthy and unfavorable circumstances. There is not enough time to organize all the data and assess possible strategies and solutions to resolve the vast array of needs.

Forecasting that AI, AGI, nanotechnology and molecular manufacturing may resolve many of these needs, transhumanists evoked a future that could be healthy and favorable for all. In the 1990s, this was considered science fiction and frivolous by some bioethicists and environmentalists. However, today (within a different intellectual climate), there are entrepreneurs who see the potential of these technologies. For example, K. Eric Drexler wrote *Engines of Creation* in 1986 about nanotechnology and a future of rearranging matter to supplant the needs of many—housing, clean water, food, medical care. "We need to develop and spread an understanding of the future as a whole, as a system of interlocking dangers and opportunities. This calls for the effort of many minds. ... The coming years will bring the greatest turning point in the history of life on Earth" (Drexler, 1986, p. 239). Why? Because, "[o]ur ability to arrange atoms lies at the foundation of technology" (Drexler, 1986, p. 3).

Peter Diamandis, founder of the X Prize Foundation, in *Abundance: The Future Is Better Than You Think* (Diamandis and Kotler, 2014) writes "Scarcity has been an issue since life first emerged on this planet ..." (p. 6). "There are now more than seven billion people on this planet. If trends don't reverse, by 2050, we'll be closer to ten billion" (p. 7). And at the end of the section on "Our Grandest Challenge", the final comments are: "But acting together, amplified by exponentially growing technologies, the once-unimaginable becomes the now actually possible" (p. 11). The natural response—so, what is possible?

Transhumanism—a worldview where people inspire each other to create, to innovate, to challenge the unknown, and to be explorers of the future.

Fair enough. Yet, to achieve this goal the first hurdle to overcome was the transhumanist claim that the "human condition" needed to be changed. That claim caused a bit of backlash in the 1990s because of modernist social standards of identifying and defining "normal" state of existence for humans based on size, shape, race, IQ, gender, etc. Outside the fine lines of what was accepted as normal, a person was either slow and at a mental disadvantage or smart with a high IQ. However, the criteria for assessing the data was not as advanced as one would hope. People were put into categories and assumed to perform based on the establish criteria per category. Certainly, there were outliers, but they were often discarded as unusual.

As a second point for the misinterpretation of transhumanist goals, the postmodernist academics and its social standards that countered modernist thought were unaware of the entrepreneurs, scientists and technologies that were seeking solutions to the human condition. As repercussion, postmodernists associated transhumanism with dystopian science fiction. This misassumption was largely due to a lack of first-hand empirical experience of the future studies and the escalating technological innovations that were occurring.

Also, the transhumanist movement has had to overcome harsh criticism of the press that associated it with science fiction narrative and futurist scenarios that were embellished with disembodied brains—as uploads. Nothing could have been further from the truth. Transhumanists in the 1990s were often vitamin-taking purveyors who were researching life extension and encryption, life extensionists who pursued computer science and/or philosophy and the future, while delving into encryption, blockchain, cybersecurity, nanotechnology, 3D printing, genetics, etc. et al.

When the 21st century arrived, most of the early ideas of transhumanists had become mainstream, and some of the naysayers, such as Francis Fukyama and Leon Kass, whose bioethicist salvos had impeded the progress of research and investigation of stem cells, had finally falling behind and people were becoming informed through talking with others throughout the world and finding answers to their own questions. The Internet afforded people with not only knowledge, but with hope that we could change the world for the better.

Movement

It is difficult to estimate the number of transhumanists worldwide. It is safe to say in the thousands if not more. There are numerous transhumanist organizations, projects, and events. Some transhumanists are located in the technologies and work at advancing encryption, cryptocurrencies, security, and focus on areas of personal identity. Other transhumanists are located in the sciences and research and develop projects that engage life extension therapies and the prevention of disease. Areas that are often filled with transhumanists are nutrition and exercise. Others enjoy science fiction and write expansive narratives on what the future might be like in a fictional sense. Others are more aligned with serious fiction and are strategists, futurists, and entrepreneurs who assess the decades ahead and alternative scenarios for humanity, including those that engage AGI, supercomputers, automation, and robotics, and the potential for a technological singularity.

There is a large formation of political transhumanists who consider the governance—laws, policies and legislation—of their countries as crucial to the transhumanist agenda. Along these lines of thinking, bioethicists and machine ethicists are of interest to many transhumanists whose debating skills are highly beneficial to the movement. The philosophical and theoretical fields are also well-seated by transhumanists who identify and analyze the issues humanity is facing, existential risks, and what we might become.

1980s

Transhuman conferences
UCLA offers courses on Transhuman
"Transhuman Manifesto" published
TV program "Breakthroughs Transhuman TransCentury UPdate" airs
Extropy: Journal of Transhumanist Thought published

1990s

Philosohpy or Transhumanism authored
Extropy Institute incorporates
Extropy email list
Extro Conferences
Aleph (Sweden)
Transhumanist FAQ published
Transcedo (Netherlands
De:Trans (Europe)
TransVision Conference held by Transcedo
TransVision Conference held by Aleph
De:Trans (Germany)

THEORY & PRACTICE
Proactionary Principle
Morphological Freedom
Technoprogressive
Transpolitics/Transpolitica

2000s

WTA incorporates
Journal of Transhumanist Thought published
EXI Vital Progress Summit
Italian Transhumanist Association
Association Francaise Transhumaniste Technoprog
WTA rebrands to Humanity+
h+ Magazine published
H+ Summits
Mormon Transhumanist Association
Humanity+@ Conferences
H+Pedia
Christian Transhumanist Association
Association Transhumanista Latino Americana

ONGOING
H+ Chapter growth
H+ Education
H+ Policy Making

CHAPTER 2

Where did it come from?

Who first used the term or coined it. No one knows.

The central and spirited ideas of transhumanism can be traced to thought-provoking writings about a potential transition and transformation of the human species in overcoming odds. These forecasts have appeared at different times and with different meanings.

The term transhuman has an unusual etymology in that its usage is found within the fields of literature, philosophy, religion, evolutionary biology. The "Report on The Meaning of Transhuman" (Vita-More, 1989) uncovered the first known reference to the transhumanism written by poet Dante Alighieri in his magnum opus *Paradiso of the Divina Commedia* (1312). It is in this masterpiece, Dante wrote the world "transhumanized" to describe what happens to humans through a "beatific vision." In this reference, trans-human means "go outside the human condition and perception". The English translation is "to transhumanate" or "to transhumanize".

Centuries later, poet T.S. Eliot used the term "transhumanized" to represent the risks of the human journey in becoming illuminated as a "process by which the human is Transhumanised" in "The Cocktail Party" (1949). What is unusual, is that both authors, centuries apart, were poets.

Evolutionary biologist Julian Huxley wrote about how humans must establish a better environment for themselves in the essay "Transhumanism" in *New Bottles For New Wine* (1957). Another finding of the term was by French engineer Jean Coutrot in 1939, although the specific writings are not yet uncovered.

A link is found between T.S. Eliot and Teilhard de Chardin, a philosopher and a Catholic priest, who proposed that man use any appropriate means for transhumanizing himself to the fullest potential in *The Future of Man* (1959).

The term transhuman was formally identified and codified in *The Reader's Digest Great Encyclopedia Dictionary*, which defined "transhuman" as meaning "surpassing; transcending; beyond" (1966). Almost a decade later, science fiction borrowed the concept with Robert Ettinger's use of the term transhumanity in *Man into Superman.* (1972). Futurist FM Esfandiary introduced the future of human evolution in his chapter "Transhumans 2000" in *Women the Year 2000* (Tripp, 1974).

The interpretation of the transhuman as an evolutionary process was noted in *Webster's New Universal Unabridged Dictionary*, which defined "transhuman" as meaning "superhuman," and "transhumanize," as meaning "to elevate or transform to something beyond what is human" (1983). At that same time, I authored the "Transhuman Manifesto" (Vita-More, 1983), emphasizing an aim to transcend the limits of our bodies and our minds.

There are numerous forbearers of theories on human evolution and traces can be found in a plethora of sources, all suggesting that the biological human is not the final stage of evolution. The philosophy, worldview, and social/cultural movement of transhumanism has developed not only from the words "trans" and "human", but also through an understanding that the human condition is one in which we might go outside to gain perspective, a process in becoming, an evolutionary transformation.

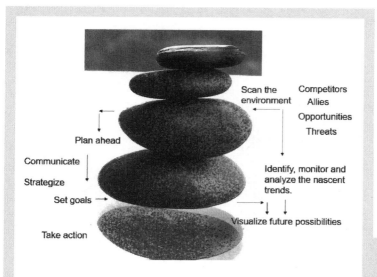

Scan the environment

Competitors
Allies
Opportunities
Threats

Plan ahead

Communicate

Strategize

Identify, monitor and analyze the nascent trends.

Set goals

Visualize future possibilities

Take action

CHAPTER 3

How uncertain
is the future?

Very uncertain. But this not a bad thing! The future has always been uncertain for the present because it has not happened yet. How do we live in a state of calmness and confidence in a world of uncertainty? By learning how to think about the future. Change is a natural process. The aim is to learn how to think about the future and to accept and even enjoy the challenges of a changing world.

Do you want to live in a world where people have more empathy, more humanness? Do you want to see poverty disappear and everyone, everywhere living a productive life in good health? Do you want to travel into space and explore the Earth's Solar System and beyond? Are you satisfied with your well-being and healthiness or would you prefer to be more joyous and at maximum health, living as long as you desire? Would you enjoy experiencing life within multiple substrates and platforms—exist in this material, physical biological world and also a virtual and artificial environment, similar to the film *Avatar*?

Who will benefit from the future?

I am often asked about the "haves" and the "have nots" based on a deep concern of people that there will be an elite class of people that are enhance and acquire superlongevity (radical life extension) and other show will be left behind—humans of antiquity. In my view this is an issue we need to address now but may not be an issue we will have in the future because the advocacy for exponential technology and for humanness override the current lack of supplies for people in need.

Outside of narratives science fiction that has spoon-fed society with a dystopic version of the future, we do have real issues that need to be addressed. Every day I am amazed that there are people in the world that do not have food or housing. Why? Is not because of an elite society in developed countries that others in developing countries suffer. It is because of a sociopathic behavior of governing bodies, institutions, and leaders who cause the problem. Those in the global society who are working and to build a culture of healthy, long lives are largely transhumanist and other life extensionists who care about all of humanity, along with those who are developing cures for disease and the technology to expedite the cures. We all know that there are people across our planet who need clean water, medical supplies and housing.

Inequality: haves and have nots

Wealth distribution is based on the economic structures.

- Some governments support the ability of a person to create a company, produce a product, and sell it. Competition keeps the marketplace in balance. A new company may arise and produce the product at a lower cost and higher quality, and it will become successful and the earlier company may go out of business. (an economic and political system in which a country's trade and industry are controlled by private owners for profit, rather than by the state.)

- Some governments support the ability of a person to create a company but gets a kickback. In some areas a large kickback. Thus, the company make just enough money to sustain in a state of poverty.

- Some governments support mutually voluntary dependence on money from others (governments and charities) (socialism).

Superlongevity and Elitists

- Superlongevity: The financial status of a person who eats well, exercises, meditates, and work with a purpose in life do not equal a wealthy elite. These are two separate issues. A wealthy person can be foolish, fat, and not live long due to a lack of self-care.

- Superlongevity: The cost of living longer will come down as the marketplace produces products at a lower cost and higher quality. This is the historical behavior of industry, competition, and progress.

- Antique Homo Sapiens: This would only occur if a person determines that they want to remain an antique—100% biological human with no enhancements. It will be a personal choice. The theory of Morphological Freedom comes into play here: a person has the right to enhance and live longer. Equally, a person has the right never to be coerced to enhance and live longer. This will become a fundamental human and transhuman right globally.

Previously I stated that the "haves" and "have nots" is an issue we need to be concerned with now, but may not be an issue we will have to deal with in the future. This is because the potential advances in technology (e.g., molecular engineering) and automation, supplies will be made at a faster pace and delivered to people around the world without intervention of governing bodies that prevent their own people from receiving help. We have seen this with countries throughout the world where people are literally starving and suffering because their governing bodies are less than humane.

In short, rather than this awful and deeply sad situation where people are suffering because of lack of clean water, housing, cloths, medical supplies, food, etc. imagine a future where automation could produce products at a nano-cost and deliver to people independently. Getting to people is challenging, and channels for delivery of good is necessary. But rather than having to deal with theft at boarders, molecular manufacturing can build products on the spot where products are needed—housing, food, cloths, clean water, etc. That future is not tomorrow, but the vision is here today, and that vision will come to fruition. We made it to the moon and we can make it to people in need.

ARTIFICIAL INTELLIGENCE IS ESSENTIAL

WHY?

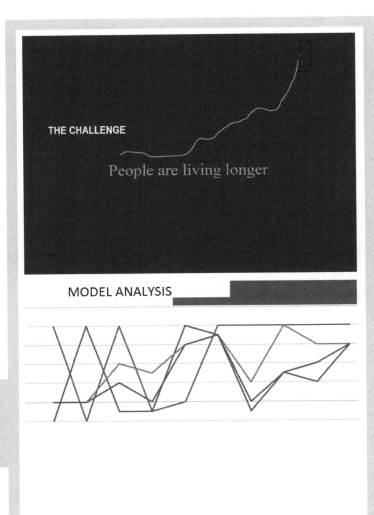

THE CHALLENGE

People are living longer.

MODEL ANALYSIS

CHAPTER 4

What challenges do we face?

Cybersecurity

Personal identity and financial security are at risk. Outside the sphere of individual well-being, government institutions are at risk. Due to a lack of technicians in the fields of cybersecurity (network security, network engineering, and technology forensics), grant funders are soliciting for programs to get students into the field, early—starting at the K12 level through 2-year colleges, 4-year degree programs, and at the graduate level. The area where we are seeing a large gap is in vulnerability testing, analysis and recording. Vulnerability testing is how cybersecurity technicians can identify breaches in security and develop protocols for securing the breaches. Much of this work is based on analytics and recording such information. Without the records of how breaches are made by hackers and recording methods for securing information, there is no model or practice to implement. Without training students to be cybersecurity technicians, the world is facing hacking from anyone, anywhere, anytime. Our personal and governing institutions information is at risk.

Terrorists: Death is the Worst

The greatest threat to human life is disease. The second greatest threat are humans. In the future the largest threat may be AGI, but today the concern is staying alive long enough to live indefinitely. In a world where terrorism, the unlawful use of force or violence against persons or property to intimidate or coerce a government, civilians, or any segment of society, a transhumanist agenda would be to steer clear of areas in the world where terrorism is heavy. However, it is now everywhere—shopping malls, nightclubs, even on the streets of London and Paris. There may not be much we can do to stop terrorism, but there is much we can do to stop disease and the all too soon death, and if humans do evolve to be more humane, then humans might not be influenced to force their political, religious, or ideological values onto others.

Financial stability

Cut up the credit cards. Use cash and stop spending money that you do not have. If we are going to live longer, then we need to have a financial plan for our own financial stability. The average 2017 household in the US had a credit card dept of $15,482, while Americans' total credit card debt was estimated at $927 million (El Issa, 2017). Because of the changes in retirement age, benefits, and economic stability worldwide, each of us needs to have a plan of action. To begin, identify your needs, the basics of food, healthcare, housing. Consider not retiring and going back to school (lifelong learning) online for free or for a small percentage of the cost of most universities.

Overpopulation

For this section, I defer to Max More's seminal essay on "Super-longevity Without Overpopulation":

"The share of the global population accounted for by the developed nations has fallen from 32 percent in 1950 to 20 percent currently and is projected to fall to 13 percent in 2050. If we look just at Europe, we see an even more remarkable shrinkage: In 1950, Europe accounted for 22 percent of the global population. Currently it has fallen to 13 percent and is projected to fall to 7 percent by 2050. To put this in perspective, consider that the population of Africa at 749 million is now greater than that of Europe at 729 million, according to UN figures. Europe's population growth rate of just 0.03 per cent will ensure that it will rapidly shrink relative to Africa and other developing areas.

"In Eastern Europe, population is now shrinking at a rate of 0.2 percent. Between now and 2050, the population of the more developed regions is expected to change little. Projections show that by mid-century, the populations of 39 countries will be smaller than today. Some examples: Japan and Germany 14 percent smaller; Italy and Hungary 25 percent smaller; and the Russian Federation, Georgia and Ukraine between 28-40 percent smaller. (Bjorn, 2001).

For the United States (whose population grows faster than Europe), the bottom line was summed in a presentation to the President's Council on Bioethics by S.J. Olshansky who "did some basic calculations to demonstrate what would happen if we achieved immortality today". The bottom line is that if we achieved immortality today, the growth rate of the population would be less than what we observed during the post-World War II baby boom (Olshansky, 2002).

"Low fertility means that population trends in the developed regions of the world would look even milder if not for immigration. As the 2000 Revision to the UN Population Division's projections says: 'The more developed regions are expected to continue being net receivers of international migrants, with an average gain of about 2 million per year over the next 50 years. Without migration, the population of more developed regions as a whole would start declining in 2003 rather than in 2025, and by 2050 it would be 126 million less than the 1.18 billion projected under the assumption of continued.

"All things considered, countries fortunate enough to develop and make available radical solutions to aging and death need not worry about becoming overpopulated. In an ideal scenario, life extension treatments would rapidly plunge in cost, making them affordable well beyond the richest nations. We should therefore look beyond the developed nations and examine global population trends in case a significantly different picture emerges" (More, 2004).

Existential risk

This area includes existence risk as well as other catastrophic risks that face humanity. The expert in this area is Nick Bostrom and his essay "Existential Risks: Analyzing Human Extinction Scenarios and Related Hazards". In his FAQ, Bostrom refers to the biggest existential risks today:

"The great bulk of existential risk in the foreseeable future is anthropogenic; that is, arising from human activity. In particular, most of the biggest existential risks seem to be linked to potential future technological breakthroughs that may radically expand our ability to manipulate the external world or our own biology. As our powers expand, so will the scale of their potential consequences—intended and unintended, positive and negative.

"For example, there appear to be significant existential risks in some of the advanced forms of synthetic biology, nano-technology weaponry, and machine superintelligence that might be developed later this century. There might also be significant existential risk in certain future dystopian evolutionary scenarios, simulation-shutdown scenarios, space colonization races, nuclear arms races, climate change and other environmental disturbances, unwise use of human enhancement, and in technologies and practices that might make permanent global totalitarianism more likely.

"Finally, many existential risks may fall within the category of 'unknown unknowns': it is quite possible that some of the biggest existential risks have not yet been discovered" (Bostrom, n.d.).

Technological singularity

Vernor Vinge, mathematician and science fiction author, developed the concept of the technological singularity. Below is his original writing for VISION-21 Symposium sponsored by NASA Lewis Research Center, in March of 1993:

"The acceleration of technological progress has been the central feature of this century. We are on the edge of change comparable to the rise of human life on Earth. The precise cause of this change is the imminent creation by technology of entities with greater-than-human intelligence. Science may achieve this breakthrough by several means (and this is another reason for having confidence that the event will occur):

- Computers that are 'awake' and superhumanly intelligent may be developed. (To date, there has been much controversy as to whether we can create human equivalence in a machine. But if the answer is 'yes,' then there is little doubt that *more* intelligent beings can be constructed shortly thereafter.)

- Large computer networks (and their associated users) may "wake up" as superhumanly intelligent entities.

- Computer/human interfaces may become so intimate

that users may reasonably be considered superhumanly intelligent.

- Biological science may provide means to improve natural human intellect.

"The first three possibilities depend on improvements in computer hardware. Actually, the fourth possibility also depends on improvements in computer hardware, in an indirect way.

"Progress in hardware has followed an amazingly steady curve in the last few decades. Based on this trend, I believe that the creation of greater-than-human intelligence will occur during the next thirty years. (Charles Platt has pointed out that AI enthusiasts have been making claims like this for thirty years. Just so I'm not guilty of a relative-time ambiguity, let me be more specific: I'll be surprised if this event occurs before 2005 or after 2030" (Vinge, 1993).

Raymond Kurzweil made the technological singularity a household name when he authored *The Singularity is Near: When Humans Transcend Biology* (2006). In an explanation that is plausible, Kurzweil sets out the meaning of the singularity:

"It's a future period during which the pace of technological change will be so rapid, its impact so deep, that human life will be irreversibly transformed. Although neither utopian nor dystopian, this epoch will transform the concepts that we rely on to give meaning to our lives, from our business models to the cycle of human life, including death itself" (p. 7).

AI / AGI

John McCarthy coined the term "artificial intelligence" in 1955; however, the often-referred to father of artificial intelligence is attributed to Marvin Minsky. When McCarthy determined to develop criteria for a field of study about thinking machines, he approached the Rockefeller Foundation for funding a seminar at Dartmouth College, where he was an Assistant Professor. On September of 1955, ten computer scientists and information theoreticians, proposed a study that introduce ed the term 'artificial intelligence'. In 1958 McCarthy and Minsky created the Artificial Intelligence Group at Massachusetts Institute of Technology (MIT). As one of the most distinguished scientific enterprises in the world (Bernstein, 1981).

There are varied levels or types of AI, depending on a distinction between problem solving or reasoning tasks and cognitive abilities including self-awareness: narrow AI, weak AI, strong AI, and A general I. Sapient AI can think and reason, but it is not sentient if it cannot experience emotions and feel pain or joy, for example.

Currently the field of artificial general intelligence (AGI), coined by Ben Goertzel, or strong AI is what the buzz is all about—will this cause an extinction risk for humanity? Elon Musk, the late Stephen Hawking, and Bill Gates, and others, brought this to our attention over the past few years with claims that AI could end the human race. In an open letter on artificial intelligence, as a salvo calling for focused research on social impacts of AI:

"The potential benefits (of AI) are huge, since everything that civilization has to offer is a product of human intelligence; we cannot predict what we might achieve when this intelligence is magnified by the tools AI may provide, but the eradication of disease and poverty are not unfathomable. Because of the great potential of AI, it is important to research how to reap its benefits while avoiding potential pitfalls" (Future of Life Institute, 2015).

Not all computer scientists and machine ethicists agree. Evidence that the field of AI is growing in well-known in academics and the business sector, which needs smarter AI programming. The fear is whether or not AGI will threaten humanity by being smarter, more capable, and advanced than humans. The benefit is that humanity cannot, in my view, survive and evolve to sustain our species without it. Goertzel writes effectively about this topic as the person who first used the term AGI and the organizers of international conferences on AGI. His book *AGI Revolution: An Inside View of the Rise of Artificial General Intelligence* (Goertzel, 2016) helps set out a formidable understanding of AI's future and also addresses the topic of the technological singularity—from Kurzweil's exponential rise to a transhumanist moderate perspective of incremental surges over time.

Without AI humanity cannot solve the problems of today and most likely not tomorrow. To solve problems, strategic analytics and analysis is necessary to scrutinize data and develop scenarios. The timely aspect of this process is the collection of data. The more data that is collected the better we can understand and uncovered that need to be resolved. Yet, the amount of time and energy to do this is exhaustive. AI and the more advanced AI becomes, the better it will deliver strategic analyses for us to render decisions.

The principle develops a pan critical understanding of the diversity of those involved in radical life extension. It forms a foundation for varied views and social interactions. This foundation establishes a specific goal to understand information within and around the culture of life extension

This goal encourages evidence-based science, innovative technology, ethical standards, positive thinking, and global

BODY COMPARISON CHART

Traditional Body

Limited Life span
Legacy genes
Wears out
Makes random mistakes
Single viewpoint
Gender restriction
Prone to environmental damage
Emotional distress

Future Body

Ageless
Replaceable genes
Upgrades
Error correction
Multiple parallel viewpoints
Gender changeability
Impervious to environmental damage
Turbocharged practical optimism

Built to last, engineered to adapt.

CHAPTER 5

Will humans evolve and, if so, into what?

Humans will evolve but no one knows what we will evolve into. There are trajectories that the human will become a human in transition or transhuman and later become posthuman. The posthuman is suggested to be a person who can co-exist in multiple substrates, such as the physical world as a biological or semi-biological being. The future human, whatever it will be called, will live much longer than a human and most likely travel outside the Earth's orbit.

Evolutionary biologist Lyn Margulis authored an answer to one of the most unknown questions that humanity has faced: What is Life? In her book *What is Life?* (Margulis and Sagan, 2000), the authors bring us directly into bodily matter as an evolutionary conglomeration of bacterial strains where life is "the transmutation of energy and matter" (p. 215) in performing an autopoietic behavior. Margulis' proposed theory of "symbiogenesis" suggests that humans are comprised of a conglomerate of life forms—that as animals, humans are nucleated cells descended not just from a Darwinian theory of natural selection and common ancestry, but from ancient bacteria, which themselves comprise different strains of bacteria. The idea of a symbiogenesis becomes an underlying theme throughout the Margulis study and inspired what I call a "biotechnogenesis" of emerging and exponential technologies, which form the media of life extension and expansion.

Human Evolution

For clarification and objectivity, I defer to the Smithsonian Institute's Introduction to Human Evolution:

"Scientific evidence shows that the physical and behavioral traits shared by all people originated from apelike ancestors and evolved over a period of approximately six million years. ...

"One of the earliest defining human traits, bipedalism -- the ability to walk on two legs -- evolved over 4 million years ago. Other important human characteristics -- such as a large and complex brain, the ability to make and use tools, and the capacity for language -- developed more recently. Many advanced traits -- including complex symbolic expression, art, and elaborate cultural diversity -- emerged mainly during the past 100,000 years. ...

"Most scientists currently recognize some 15 to 20 different species of early humans. Scientists do not all agree, however, about how these species are related, or which ones simply died out. Many early human species -- certainly the majority of them – left no living descendants. Scientists also debate over how to identify and classify particular species of early humans, and about what factors influenced the evolution and extinction of each species" (Smithsonian National Museum of Natural History, n.d.).

All life on earth is continually evolving. Human physiological characteristic: skull size, jaw, brain size, and teeth are different than our ancestors; yet, the evolution is not shocking or divergent. We have a maximum life span of an approximately 123 years and that has not changed. Most humans live longer because of medical interventions and social standards Nevertheless, thousands of human genes have evolved over the last 40,000 years (Forbes, 2016).

"Countering a common theory that human evolution has slowed to a crawl or even stopped in modern humans, a new study examining data from an international genomics project describes the past 40,000 years as a time of supercharged evolutionary change, driven by exponential population growth and cultural shifts" (Mattmiller, 2007).

That the convergent—emerging and exponential technologies of genetic engineering, Crispr, stem cells, nanomedicine, and other techniques, along with cellular rejuvenation and immunotherapies could extend the human life span beyond its limits and, further, alter the genome, reverse the effects of aging, increase intelligence, and possibly bring about a species' evolution of the homo sapiens toward transformation of transhuman and later toward a type of posthuman future, then it is likely that here where a social and cultural tension resides. This tension pulls us in the direction of curiosity and intrigue in exploring where these possible changes could lead us, and it yanks us away abruptly, as if having confronted a border tainted with historical angst, mythical warnings, religious improprieties, ethical concerns, and socio-political disappointments and confusions.

Bioethics: Objective logic?

This depends on the bioethicist. There are some who are objective and open-mined and others who rely on their moral compass.

Leon Kass, physician and former chairman of President George W. Bush's Council on Bioethics presented "Defending Human Dignity" at the 2007 Bradley Lecture Series at the Wohlstetter Conference Center in Washington, DC. It is evident that Kass fears that a biotechnological quest to satisfy "venerable human desires" (Bailey 2007) will lead ultimately to humanity's self-degradation—that it will cause humans to lower the collective dignity and, therefore, in our attempt to become more than human we actually will end up "less than human" (2007).

Kass complains about harvesting organs, but isn't it moral and laudatory to donate one's organs for use as transplants? Kass warns against 'mechanical spare parts,' but what could possibly be immoral about an artificial knee or hip? People are certainly not choosing to use biomedical therapies such as the birth control pill, in vitro fertilization and even Viagra so that they can produce standard men and women. Kass' colleague Francis Fukuyama asserts that there is a human factor must not be tampered with. For Fukuyama humans contain what he refers to as the "Factor X", a type of essential human quality that must be protected and preserved from potential methods and approaches that might affect—or redefine—the factor, such as through the work of biotechnology.

However, what is this Factor X? Could this be an essential evolutionary genetic shift that separated man from earlier species? Fukuyama does not spell out this Factor X in a way that clarifies what he is saying and, perhaps, he is not quite sure himself, but it is something he senses is as crucial as human nature—if not human dignity itself—and which he leaves to historical human biology. Thus, tampering with, altering and modifying the essential genes of humans would tarnish this yet-to-be-understood Factor X, even if such alternations and modifications were to remove, for example, a set of inherited genes that code an inevitably devastating disease. Thus, one might ask: Where is the dignity of the person who suffers from a horrific disease—a disease that is not only painful, but portends to distort his body in unimaginable ways, or alters his psychology by bringing about states of psychosis that occur abruptly and unpredictably?

There will be divides in beliefs about human evolution. However, if there is a fundamental acknowledgement and respect for human rights and individual choices, as long as one person's choice does not hurt another person or damage other life forms, then their views need to be respected and vice versa. This is the fundamental principle of Morphological Freedom for human rights.

Transhuman Future:
Existing across substrates

Video games, virtual reality, and augmented reality are platforms that people interface with and online environments are as natural as real-time. This is a mere beginning of humans co-existing in multiple substrates.

Consider the concept of human evolution where the body endures over time as a sustainable system. This system simulates biology with technology to function as an adaptive process by organizing cells, molecules, and machines to work in concert for regenerative purposes. The process of renewal, restoration and growth within this ecosystem is necessary for resilience to normal fluctuations within of biology and the environment. As such, it is only natural that the human body evolve to a state of renewal and restoration as a precaution to the imperilment of life.

The future human body is not unlike or in conflict with the classical human form or the idea of the future posthuman. Because of its transitional stage, the body is a synergistic, symbolic inter-pretation of the form in which the ultimate value is to sustain life, no matter the substrate.

An anticipated cohesiveness of identity among the human, cyborg, transhuman and posthuman is to first establish similarities between them. First, the postmodernist concept of a posthuman body is that it is not a physical, object-based system. Second, the assumption that posthuman and transhuman bodies lack a sense of unity or "oneness" – or a type of inclusivity among all agency is a false premise because no one knows the inner psychology of another, especially while asserting segregated labels. For example, a transhuman is a human in transition to becoming something other. It could be a posthuman, or not. No one knows. Never-theless, in the time frame and as a chronological order, a human comes first, then transhuman and then perhaps the posthuman. In this strategy, the cyborg has symbolic and mechanistic value. Because the cyborg has a place in academics and in cybernetics, it offers a way of considering a future human without having to attach radical life extension, the singularity, uploading, or other theories to it. Alternatively, the transhuman is deeply linked to radical life extension and the sciences and technologies that mitigate the disease of ageing, including artificial intelligence and nanomedicine. Further, the transhuman is logged in the domain of computer science and theories on backing up the brain, brain transfer, and uploading consciousness.

Yet, the transhuman arrived prior to the cyborg and they do share similar attributes, barring the previously mentioned focus of sustaining and extending human life.

Modifications to the human body are historical. Ancient roots uncover physical changes developed due to diversity of environments and environmental instability. Adapting to the surroundings influenced the body form (bipedalism) as well as the brain's complexity. While these changes evolved over considerable length of time, research claims that the homo sapiens has not changed for the past 50,000 years. However, with DNA research sequencing and deciphering content, it is evident that the evolution continues and may be accelerating rather than static (McAuliffe, 2009). Are humans evolving at the genetic level? According to the Smithsonian Institute research, "new genetic mutations arise with each generation" causing "rare genetic variants in the protein-encoding" (Shultz, 2012). To validate these claims, markers would need to be detected to identify recent evolution. Even with markers, these changes are not truly evolution but an individual adaptation. It may be that "[t]he relative importance of natural selection in shaping our species might be weak at present, but it has the potential to become stronger again in the future" (Stock, 2008).

The substrate-diverse and autonomous body, much like the human body, would rely on energy-efficient systems to function. The human body relies on mitochondria for energy, as well as a healthy microbiome that protects the human from germs and breaks down nutrients from foods. If this environment is not stable or does not respond to disturbances effectively, ill health ensues. Similar to the process the microbial communities within the human body must be maintained by restorative factors (Langdon, Crook, & Dantas, 2016), the substrate-diverse autonomous body would need regenerative processes to function. This could be electricity, solar energy, chemical reactions, and even self-propelling.

For example, it would need to be continually monitored for nanorobot efficiency as they intervene with cellular malfunctions, the central nervous system's digital interconnectivity in extracting messages, the brains error correction system, instant replay, and memory fastidiousness, the sensorial expansion of micro and telescopic vison, auditory selectiveness, the skin's proficiency in mutating instantly to environmental changes, and the brain's flow of data across substrates, and the mind's ability to coalesce data without fracturing. All these functions require the joint effort of processes that engage semi-biological and computational systems within the material world and virtual, artificial substrates. If any of these systems break down, then repair is necessary. However, the repair may not be as time-oriented as with the human body, as the disease of aging is chronological and with the transhuman, time is exponential. At any moment, the body and person could be suspended and/or reconnected.

The aim of this vehicle body would renew its system perpetually, restore and grow; with the caveat the growth is not leaner because it travels across substrates. By this, it could live in the physical, computational, digital, virtual, and artificial worlds.

Three thresholds that are currently affecting the advent of transhuman bodies include:

- Nanomedicine: Currently, nanomedicine is practices in the pharmaceutical industry for drug delivery, vaccinations, cell and gene therapy. It holds great promise, but still is largely theoretical in the vision of where it is headed and how it will influence medicine within the next decade.

- Computational Neuroscience: Currently in the theoretical and modeling stages. The goal is to construct a software model that will behave the same way as the original brain (Sandberg, 2008)

- Artificial General Intelligence. Currently, AGI is not possible. Narrow AI is largely available in all operating systems and task-oriented technologies. Methods for AGI are currently of the symbolic-AI paradigm or human-readable representations of problems (Goertzel and Pennachin, 2007).

As a vehicle for life, the body vehicle is scrutinized for its efficiency and its resistance to aging and death. As scientific research attains each new threshold, knowledge is gained that evidences an intended or unintended aim to mitigate biology with technology. In doing so, this aim further seeks to develop adaptive, resilient and sustainable bodies. Knowledge of the uses of technology to alter biology has revolutionized society and changed the way people think about their own DNA. This change in thinking must also include advances in human psychology. It is a natural urge to further evolution with intelligence that evolves from hypercriticality and other cognitive biases and imbues internal and external awareness and understanding.

Like a maze, the number of cells within the body is beyond imagination, much like the number of stars in the universe, and within each cell is another array of data. Yet, the pragmatic focus is on durability, efficiency, and adaptiveness in sustaining life.

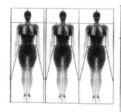

Multiple selves across substrates

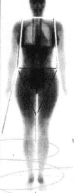

Radical Life Extension

- Are there observable problems?
- Where is it headed?
- Redesign biological system
- Examine external environment
- Investigate alternative platforms

FUTURE OF AGEING
SOCIETY OF ACHIEVERS

BODY   BRAIN   MIND

COMPUTERS

Cybernetics   BCI   eocortex
Augmentation   Hierarchy of Ideas
Body Art   Pattern Recognizers
Wearables   X-ray   Symbols
Biohacking   CAT   Patterns
Body Apps   MRI / fMRI   Complexities
                     EEG
                     MEG
                     KESM
                     SNI

HUMAN   CLOUD
ENHANCEMENT

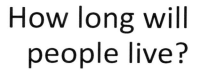

CHAPTER 6

How long will people live?

Until the cause of aging can be mitigated and reversed, into their 100s, but not past 123.5 years. But tomorrow people will live far beyond these years.

People who want to live long, healthy lives support radical life extension, also known as superlongevity and indefinite lifespans. In comparison, the phrase life extension usually refers to living a full life with the aid of diet, exercise, and vitamins to maintain good health within the maximum human lifespan, but not beyond. The phrase radical life extension is synonymous with the concepts of superlongevity and indefinite life, which mean that the human's life span can be extended well beyond the maximum biological time frame. This time frame is recorded to be approximately 122.5 years. People can live reasonably healthy lives through their 70s, 80s and 90s; yet, deterioration of bone and muscle mass advances, skin elasticity diminishes, hearing and eyesight weaken and overall physical strength declines.

Nevertheless, there are more centenarians today than ever—especially in the western world. According to Smithsonian research, in 2000 there were approximately 50,000 Americans who were over 100. In 2014, that percentage increased 44% up to over 72,000 people (Fessenden, 2016). This is the good news. The overwhelmingly bad news is that Alzheimer's and other types of dementia have increased, causing cognitive dysfunction.

Those of us who are working in the field of radical life extension need to be educated and well-informed. Just wishing for healthy, long life does not beget healthy long life. Our psychology and positive attitude are extremely important attributes to developing a radical life extension mindset, but we also need to be pragmatic about how our bodies and minds are aging. And here we have another issue to contend with: If we do extend the maximum life span well beyond 123 years and reverse the damage of ageing and return our bodies to earlier levels of strength and agility, we must perform the same engineering to increase neurological and cognitive performance.

Ageless thinking

The concept of ageless thinking addresses certain biases about aging that pigeon-hole people about age-based social constructs.

"Ageless means to be free of the characteristics associated with age. Thinking means to bring thought to mind by exercising the power of reason. Ageless thinking means to practice the exercise of thinking about maintaining a youthful state, both physically and mentally. How and what we think about age depends on our individual goals. Reasons why ageless thinking is advantageous to optimal living and refer to how ageist thinking shortens our life. Society is often imprisoned by stereotypical beliefs about aging that categorize how a person looks and how they out to act based on their age. Breaking free of these constraints allows for new models of aging that free us to imagine what we might look like and possibilities for deeper insights into our own psychology, learning, behaviors and purpose in life. If the aim is to extend life indefinitely, the corollary aim is to extend the quality of life to new heights" (Vita-More, 1996).

Through this framework, I researched assumptions that cause people to be ageists even if their inference is not intentional. I also analyzed different types of aging and with ways in which a person could practice ageless thinking, which are largely brain exercises for memory and performing new cognitive tasks. For example, training the brain to carve new thinking modalities to strengthen habits through repetitive thinking, feeling, and emotional behaviors. For my empirical research for building plasticity in thinking and challenging my own thinking process, I enrolled in two different university graduate programs and earned degrees in fields that contrasted my prior academics. This allowed me to stretch outside or beyond the framework I had previously been trained to think within. As related to ageless thinking, a transhumanist approach could be lifelong learning or a transhumanist.edu.

While ageless thinking may no longer be a social issue because of cultural awareness about ageist bias, there will be new biases to overcome. Some of these may relate to a person who has undergone age reversal in the biological sphere or, perhaps—in the future—those who select to reside in more than one environment or substrate. For example, an upload, an avatar, or a posthuman.

Life

Living longer and healthier is a systematic, organized practice. Transhumanism seeks an ethical approach to the use of technology and evidence-based science to study and mitigate disease. As a practice, it fosters a positive attitude that values pragmatic optimism as a way of being in the world undefined by gender roles, age quantifiers, or other indoctrinated behaviors that cultures accept as normal. The main one is a rejection of limited lifespans and the social conditioning toward disease and death.

Throughout history, there have been purveyors of long life. Stretching into the archives of antiquity, the Taoists, Egyptians and other cultures sought to defy the onslaught of aging and death. Passions for radical life extension can override the tools to bring it about and this fervor has kept us pounding the pavement toward progress, as we have seen through the efforts of the early alchemists in manipulating matter, or as in Nicolai Fedorov's 1828-1903) "common task" and Jean Finot's (1856-1922) proposed "fabrication of living matter."

By focusing on the theories of transmutation of matter and reflecting upon the biochemical process of death and death's possible technological futures, one then duly notes degeneration and regeneration as a necessary process and the maximum human lifespan as impermanent and mutable. This leads to questions asking what core elements of life are to be expanded and what type of matter might we live within in this expanded realm. Thus, reviewing Aristotle's "first principle of living things" (Goertz & Taliaferro 2011, p. 19) —the psyche, and related propositions concerning the molecular components and chemistry of the human, as noted by Margulis and Fahy (below), is essential to this investigation as well as how and elements of "being" in life became a proposition that life is "the transmutation of energy and matter" (Margulis & Sagan 2000, p. 215). Ultimately, we can then visualize how biotechnogenesis fosters the emergence of new types of living systems.

If atoms are the elemental components from which all cells are derived, then why does programmed cell death occur? To answer this question, Greg Fahy advises that normal biological life requires the death of cells and the division of cells to generate new cells so that a balance is maintained in bodily sub-systems such as the digestive system, reproductive system, and pulmonary system (2008). In the adult human, more than a thousand billion cells are created every day. At the same time, an equal number of cells die through a controlled "suicide process" (Alberts, Johnson & Lewis 2002:1014), referred to as programmed cell death. In short, cells kill themselves to halt the spread of disease.

Death

Definitions of death are based on observation and prognosis in meeting certain criteria proposed by the medical doctor or qualified nurse, as the available knowledgeable authority of death. But how dead does someone have to be to be dead? A limp, cold and immobile body was once considered dead, but a person could be unconscious and reawaken either with or without technologically-assisted resuscitation. A seemingly quiet chest exhibiting stillness rather than a beating heart evidenced death, but then a heart could continue to beat so quietly as to remain unobserved or invisible to human or technical monitor. Once, a candle's still flame could determine a loss of breathing, but as with a limp body and quiet heart, then the nostrils' weakened breath might go unnoticed. Testing the pulse in dominant anterior veins of the wrist, the neck or the groin suggested a total loss of blood flow, but then a person's blood flow could resume again with a strong push on the chest, a force of oxygen into the mouth, or a slap to the face. The observation that someone whose heart, lungs and pulse have stopped functioning for a period of time is no longer considered an acceptably full and accurate diagnosis that a person has ceased to exist for all time.

Transhumanists who carefully aim to protect their lives have a Plan B for radical life extension. Knowing that anything could occur at any time, having a life insurance policy for cryonics is the best protection against death.

Redefining death

The topic of death's possible futures, noting that it has been deeply discussed with varied and conflicting beliefs in numerous fields—most especially, philosophy and science, is unknown. There are many potential directions to take when conceptualizing new modes of death and how death might be redefined. To concretize a basis of understanding, the possible futures of death would rely on the most reasonable approaches, and these approaches might lead to prolonging life and sustaining persons over time within semi- and non-biological systems. The task of redefining death to incorporate notions of optional death, reversible death, and partial death could be crucial to radical life extension. The fear of being misdiagnosed as dead can be more frightening than death itself. Medical technologies now provide microscopic determinants of death, although the misdiagnosis of death is possible. I do not intend this to be a diversion, but to offer an insight into a growing concern about how and when a person is actually dead. For example, a person might have a biological death but continue, immediately or sequentially, to exist in another substrate, such as in cryonics. Notably, this might be looked at as a transformative or transitional stage of life, relying heavily on emerging and speculative technologies to reverse death.

Death as an in-between state is the technological process of cryonic preservation. Cryonics [or biostasis] is the speculative practice of using cold temperatures to preserve the life of a person who can no longer be supported by ordinary medicine. The goal is to carry the person forward through time … until the preservation process can be reversed, and the person restored to full health. Biostasis is predicated upon three assumptions: (1) that life can be stopped and restarted, as observed in embryos routinely preserved in cold temperatures which completely stop the chemistry of life, and then are restarted; (2) that vitrification (i.e., low temperatures but not freezing) can preserve biological structure through the high concentration of cryoprotectants which permits cell tissue to be cool without the formation of ice particles, and (3) methods for repairing cells at the molecular level have constituted the high probability of effective nanomedicine rather than as idle fantastical notions of science fiction. Theoretically, cryonics regards death as an event which can be prevented.

A possible future scenario might be that death not be compulsory but instead stand as a possible option, thereby leaving the act of death as a choice. Optional death might be used as a type of retirement from one life mode to another life mode. More specifically, a person existing in a synthetic simulation might decide that this environment no longer is satisfactory and determine to cease to exist in synthetic form and transfer his existence into a semi-biological material body. Another example might be where a person hosting multiple identities, each being a self-contained aspect of the person, experiences voluntarily or involuntarily cessation of existence, but this does not terminate the entirety of the person. Alternatively, death might be considered a means to drop out of life for a period of time and cease to exist indefinitely but not in finality or irrevocability.

Persons who exist outside the boundaries of the biological body will most likely desire to be considered living beings with certain rights. Therefore, it is apt to consider post-biological definitions of death concerning personhood. If medical science and technology develop the means to remediate brain dead patients, including the brain stem and neocortex, and cognitive engineering technologies develop the means to transfer memory and thought to alternative platforms for hosting life, it is reasonable to speculate that the definition of death will require a close re-examination of its operational parameters.

Activism for life

Nowhere has the depth and breadth of cultural activism, writings, talks, documentaries, and other public appearances been made or recognized outside the transhumanist movement. It is here the culture of radical life extension, superlongevity, and/or indefinite lifespans was seeded, nurtured and sprouted. As a brief history about the activism, the World Wide Web's first email list on this topic was hosted in 1991 by Extropy Institute. The numerous conferences, seminars, meetups and festivities were the result of a growing mindset that engaged all types of life extensionists who sought either a healthy long life and those who were actively pursuing the sciences and technologies that could extend the maximum span toward a far longer, radical lifespan. Along this line of thinking, was the concept of uploading, brain transfer and memory back-up as a precaution to the documented advances in memory loss and dementia.

Within the culture, knowledge about life extension is largely due to the leadership of people and their organizations dating back to the 1960s. Robert Ettinger authored *The Prospect of Immortality* (1964), Timothy Leary who wrote about SMI2LE (space migration increased intelligence, life extension) in *Exo-Psychology* (1977), FM Esfandiary approaching the topic of eliminating death as a radical approach in *Optimism One* (1978), Durk Pearson and Sandy Shaw authored *Life Extension: A Practical Scientific Approach* (1983); and Roy Walford authored *Maximum Life Span* (1985).

There have been numerous books about life extension since this time frame and these are just some of the pioneers of scientific and philosophical research that has set a foundation for others who seek technological advances and evidence-based science as an approach to reversing the damage of aging. There are pioneering organizations as well. Alcor Life Extension Foundation was incorporated in 1972 and has become the largest world known cryonics organization. Two of its members, who are well-known leaders in the life extension movement, Saul Kent and Bill Faloon developed the Life Extension Foundation (LEF) in 1980 as a nonprofit dedicated to finding breakthrough scientific methods for eradicating disease and death. LEF has become one of the largest organizations of its kind in the world, with a 38-year track record of scientific achievements in health and longevity.

In 1983, the trailblazing "Lake Tahoe Life Extension Festival" was launched in the mountains of Lake Tahoe, California and hosted by Alcor founders Fred and Linda Chamberlain. In the 1990s, the Extro 3 Conference, held in Silicon Valley (1997) focused on "The Future of Body and Brain". Two years later, the Extro 4 conference held at the University of California Berkeley (1999), focused on "Biotech Futures: Challenges of Life Extension and Genetic Engineering".

But it was not until the 2004 "Vital Progress Summit" that leaders came together to discuss the biggest issue facing life extension—governance: the FDA, Laws and Legislation that have been and could potentially be a threat to radical life extension. Scientific, technological, and cultural thinkers exchanged ideas about working to improve the world's understanding of biotechnology and science of human enhancement to improve and extend life. The Summit presented a 2-week virtual discussion and debate about President Bush's Bioethics Council's ultraconservative "Beyond Therapy Report". Summit keynotes [1] addressed the use of the well-known "Precautionary Principle" by anti-biotech activists as a rallying tool to turn people against the science, medicine and biotechnology that could cure disease and improve life.

"We have a responsibility to protect ourselves, our children and our loved ones in determining what choices to make about the future of our health. We must research and develop ethical means for the investigations of emergent sciences and technologies of human enhancement. No one has the right to tell any human that he or she must go into the later years of life in crippled or feeble states with no resolve. No organization, no policy, no person should have the absolute power and authority to hinder scientific and medical advances that can and do help millions of people throughout the world. Yet it is our responsibility to seek out ways to make sure that ethics is primary and human enhancement is available to all the seek it" (Vita-More, 2004).

The outcome of this first-time collaboration to address governance of life extension was a series of keynote statements that formed the basis of the Proactionary Principle, which was motivated by a need to make wise decisions about the development of new technologies as an ethical and decision-making principle:

"People's freedom to innovate technologically is highly valuable, even critical, to humanity. This implies a range of responsibilities for those considering whether and how to develop, deploy, or restrict new technologies. Assess risks and opportunities using an objective, open, and comprehensive, yet simple decision process based on science rather than collective emotional reactions. Account for the costs of restrictions and lost opportunities as fully as direct effects. Favor measures that are proportionate to the probability and magnitude of impacts, and that have the highest payoff relative to their costs. Give a high priority to people's freedom to learn, innovate, and advance" (More, 2005).

For the public who have a high-level of knowledge or are just learning about science and technology, Life Extension Foundation (LEF) also produces *Life Extension Magazine*. Alcor Life Foundation has been a source of information through its conferences, research program, and *Cryonics* magazine. Many Alcor members are recognized leaders of the most sophisticated scientific and technological medical processes for preserving life.

Taking place every year since 2013 is the Longevity Month, celebrated by anyone, anywhere and at specific gatherings such as the International Society on Aging and Disease conference and the TransVision conference. Another event that looks at longevity and the future is Future Day, as set out by Ben Goertzel:

"In late 2010, at the Humanity+ Leadership gathering in Second Life, I put forth the suggestion of a new holiday to celebrate the future – Future Day. After all, I noted, most of our holidays celebrate stuff from the past – why not have a holiday to celebrate the future? … Why not focus more of our attention on the future? We don't want to forget our roots. But we need to pay more attention to the important truth that those who do not pay serious attention to their future, have much less chance of affecting it in accordance with their tastes, values and ideals. This is the serious theme underlying Future Day. Let's have fun exploring all the possibilities of the future, plausible and speculative, serious and non. And let's do our best to nudge the world to refocus its attention the future and all the possibilities it holds – and our power to shape the future, together" (Goertzel, 2012).

Numerous festivals, conferences, and ways to meet others who share the same or similar interests. TED, SENS, Alcor, Humanity+, Voice & Exit, TransVision, Foresight, RAADFest, 4GameChangers, and the list goes on. But it is rare to find a conference or festival where people who all want the same thing – good health and long life.

Humanity+ has created the "H+ Prize" for innovative projects about humanity's future. The first prize was known as the "Blockchain Prize" with the topic "Mutual Benefits of Blockchain and Transhumanism", sponsored by Hadrien Majoie. Another prize that is valued is the "Longevity Film Competition", sponsored by SENS Research Foundation, The healthy Life Extension Society, and the International Longevity Alliance.

Being an activist, producer, and sponsor bring great rewards— most notably purposefulness. As we continue to development projects that help spread information everyone gains something of value. No matter the type of conference of festival, month or day, we all can be leaders and introduce the meaning of radical life extension, superlongevity and/or indefinite lifespans.

Strategic leadership

Observing how the past influences the future and the links between ideas and actions, there is gap that needs to be filled. We have witnessed the content of conference talks on the future and life extension for many decades and time is passing by. Action must be taken. Certainly, we can continue to speak at conferences that are not associated with life extension and introduce ideas about life extension, but so many people are doing that now. Googling "life extension conferences" receives 29,400,000 results and not all of them related to the events mentioned in this article.

There is a need a worldwide assemblage of activists and experts to help spread positive news, reliable information, and a well-thought-out socio-political stance. Humanity+, as a 501(c)3 nonprofit organization can steer this forward. We have the experience, passion, and the leadership skills.

Establishing a world assembly or summit (which can be virtual) to discuss human rights, laws and policies that are and will continue to affect our efforts to live longer is crucial. The contributors could be organizations and their leadership who have a track record in science, technology, psychology, philosophy, ethics, arts and humanities, and governance. The model could be similar but more advanced than the Vital Progress Summit of 2004 where we build out the Proactionary Principle. Humanity+ is skilled at organizing events, considering our conferences at Harvard, Caltech, Parson's School of Design NYC, Beijing, Hong Kong, United Kingdom, Second Life, and Spain. We also have a strong focus on AI/AGI because it is consequential for radical life extension.

Momentous to life extension is mainstream acceptance, academic scholarship, and entertainment narratives that represent real world scenarios that enlighten rather than scare the public about AI, cyborgs, avatars, transhuman, posthumans and uploads. This awareness ties into the many of the tenets that Humanity+ values, such as morphological freedom, the Proactionary Principle, and Technoprogressive socio-political views.

And considering how ideas are generated and where they were seeded and sprouted, the organizations who helped move the earliest life extension events forward are valued. Joint participation from high-level leadership within the sciences and technologies such as Life Extension Foundation, Alcor, SENS, 21st Century Medicine, Humanity+, Longevity for All, Coalition for Radical Life Extension, etc. et al is the goal. Society wants to know what it means to be human in a technologically enhanced world. We need our leaders—those who perform research, those in the laboratories, those who are entrepreneurs, and especially those who help to increase our awareness and educate us to be better thinkers and more apt doers.

In sum, transhumanist thinking is necessary tool for strategic planning, analysis, identifying BS, and developing knowledge that can help better decision-making. Through this, shared knowledge is our candle in the dark.

LIFE CAPITAL.
WHAT IS YOUR INVESTMENT?

CHAPTER 7

Is there a political agenda?

Yes, there are several. And some of the agendas overlap. There have been several attempts to organize transhumanists into political tribes, but it never seemed to work well. Most transhumanists are diverse and are more interested in problems solving than aligning with a political position; however, with the caveat that the positions fully supports the goals of transhumanism.

Transhuman politics are diverse and while many of us are left (liberal, socialist, Green) and some others right (Conservative, Libertarian), others are independent. No matter left or right all these political views are democratic transhumanists. Transhuman or Transhumanist politics is currently focused on a collaborative perspective. Most transhumanists today align with Technoprogressive politics, as outlined in its Declaration. There are also groups that have formed parties such as the US Transhumanist Party, chaired Gennady Stolyarov II, the Transhuman Party co-owned by a group of internationals, Transpolitica steered by David Wood and Chris Monteiro, Science Party lead by Peter Xing, Transhuman National Committee run by David Kelley, John Warren and Matt Brown, Parti Transhumaniste France founded by Audrey Arendt and Olivier Nero, and the Transhumanist Party Global, led by Amon Twyman.

We need a collaboration and cooperation between people to work together to change legislation and become more involved with the political landscape of the different countries where we reside. It is crucial that Humanity+ foster programs, projects, and processes to assemble people to help them get involved and at the same time remain unassociated with any one political position, and as Hughes suggests that Humanity+ be politically agnostic. This makes sense because in the US educational nonprofits cannot advocate a political party or a political agenda.

Influencers

There have been social and political influencers within transhumanism, and the humanities continue to play a major role in the ideology of humanism and links to the worldview of transhumanism. In humanism, the democratic and ethical life stance asserts that humans have a right to give meaning to their own lives. Transhumanism encases this view but takes it further by strategizing theoretical and practice-based models that propose how humans can shape their own lives. Yet, some cases, human psychology, emotions, intelligence, and mental attitudes invite or block the ability to accept or refuse the unknown. Society in the 1980s did not accept the concept of the transhuman, and in the 1990s the idea of transhumanism was loved or hated it. Strong words to be sure, but this was prevalent. Innovators of encryption and cryptocurrencies, entrepreneurs of robotics, AI, and nanotechnology, along with space enthusiasts, life extension activists, and consciousness seekers cherished the idea of transhumanism.

Conversely, bioethicists, postmodernists, religious groups, and others were concerned about new technologies, human enhancement, and genetics loathed it. Interestingly, the science fiction cyborg, borrowed the coined term from Manfred Clynes and Nathan Kline, (1960). Rather than relevant to cybernetics and a necessity for space exploration, the cyborg became a terminator. It was borrowed again as a feminist salvo in its reinterpretation by Donna Haraway in her statement "I'd Rather be a Cyborg than a Goddess" (1991).

In reflection, a question that went unanswered is why did society accept the cyborg as a machine-man science fiction terrorist and not appreciate the actual transformation of human as the transhuman—a human with ethics and a desire to enhance with technology?

Early transhumanists were mostly located in the United States in New York, Los Angeles, and startup hubs such as Silicon Valley, in Europe and Central America. New York and LA hosted more liberal thinkers with social concerns who leaned toward the Democratic party with Libertarian philosophical influence. Computer and startup hubs, such as Silicon Valley, were largely Libertarian. Entrepreneurs who funded projects were independents, Libertarian. There were also many Democrats, Green Party members, Socialists, Upwingers, etc. In LA, most transhumanists were Upwingers (neither right nor left), stemming from F.M. Esfandiary's (aka FM2030) writings about the future and the transhuman. I want to make this point clear: early transhumanists were diverse and not representative of any one religious, anti-religious, or spiritual belief and not of any one political position or party.

Political positioning for misuse of information has damaged many cultures, including transhumanism. It conflicts with the transhumanist tenets of diversity and advancement. The continual improvement as both physical and psychological. Considering this, transhumanism cannot be one political position. That attitude is counter to the fundamental values of a systems intelligence, order, vitality and capacity and drive for improvement and the three essential elements of transhumanism: critical thinking, technological innovation, and visionary narratives.

There have been a few transhumanists in the political arena over the years. FM Esfandiary set the political stage in his book *Upwingers a Futurist Manifesto* (1977), which normative platform reached beyond the Right/Left predicament and set out a non-linear evolving view of moving upward:

> "We are at all times slowed down by the narrowness of Right-wing and Left-wing alternatives. If you are not conservative, you are liberal if not right of center you are left of it or middle of the road. Our traditions comprise no other alternatives. There is no ideological or conceptual dimension beyond conservative and liberal beyond Right and Left. ... The premises of the entire Left are indistinguishable from those of the entire Right. The extreme Left is simply a linear extension of the extreme Right. The liberal is simply a more advanced conservative. The radical Left is a more advanced liberal. ... The Right/Left establishment is fighting a losing battle. It is following in the foot-steps of earlier traditionalists who resisted the more modest breakthroughs of the past. ..." (pp21-25). (F.M. Esfandiary, 1977).

In the late 1980s until 1994, I produced and hosted a small cable TV show called "Breakthroughs: A TransCentury Update" (aka "Transhuman Update") that aired in Los Angeles and Telluride, Colorado. I interviewed innovators of emerging and speculative sciences and technologies. One benefit that came out of this was body of work is that guests talked about their future-oriented innovations and broadened the scope of the program. A side effect was that due to the cutting-edge content, a viewer nominated me to run for the 27th Senatorial District of Los Angeles County on the Green Party ticket for a seat as County Councilperson. After a few months campaigning, I was elected on a Transhumanism platform—promoting environmentalist use of technology.

From the 1990s to today, there have been groups of transhumanists of who are devoted to politics and building a substantive set of guidelines and roadmap for the future. The fact is that society must be informed issues we face that will affect society and its governance. This is a far heavier issue that right vs. left. Further there is a gap in the education of society or what is often called long-long learning, where continuing education is not only essential, it is crucial. People must keep up, learn how to use smart devices to understand where technology is heading. This includes technological advancements that are altering our lives and the scope of economic and political issues; and that governments:

> "... dramatically expanded governmental research into anti-aging therapies, and universal access to those therapies as they are developed in order to make much longer and healthier lives accessible to everybody. We believe that there is no distinction between "therapies" and "enhancement." The regulation of drugs and devices needs reform to speed their approval" (Technoprogressive Declaration, 2014).

With a focus on why transhumanism is a solution to many of the issues humanity faces, mention must be given to approaches that can help the decision-making process. I will touch on several projects conceived by thought leaders of transhumanism, its early adaptors, and in a few instances, its pioneers.

To begin, decision-making works best when it is open and balanced. It is difficult for us largely because the human interpretation of information is assessed and filtered by personal perceptions. As an example, the well-known Precautionary Principle "... is a moral and political principle which states that if an action or policy might cause severe or irreversible harm to the public or to the environment, ... the burden of proof falls on those who would take the action" (IEET, n.d.). Rather than placing the burden of proof on absolute judgement of unknown outcomes, a more balanced process for policy making in weighing the pros and cons can be achieve by using the Proactionary Principle:

"People's freedom to innovate technologically is highly valuable, even critical, to humanity. This implies a range of responsibilities for those considering whether and how to develop, deploy, or restrict new technologies. Assess risks and opportunities using an objective, open, and comprehensive, yet simple decision process based on science rather than collective emotional reactions. Account for the costs of restrictions and lost opportunities as fully as direct effects. Favor measures that are proportionate to the probability and magnitude of impacts, and that have the highest payoff relative to their costs. Give a high priority to people's freedom to learn, innovate, and advance" (More, 2005).

Another necessary and timely concept for human right is Morphological Freedom, which means "[t]he ability to alter bodily form at will through technologies such as surgery, genetic engineering, nanotechnology, uploading" (More, 1993). Ownership of one's body is championed as a human right, as expressed by Anders Sandberg of the Future of Humanity Institute, Senior Research Fellow at the Future of Humanity Institute, Oxford University:

"Morphological freedom can of course be viewed as a subset of the right to one's body. But it goes beyond the idea of merely passively maintaining the body as it is and exploiting its inherent potential. Instead it affirms that we can extend or change our potential through various means. ... Without morphological freedom, there is a serious risk of powerful groups forcing change upon us. Historically the worst misuses of biomedicine have always been committed by governments and large organizations rather than individuals. ... It hence makes sense to leave decisions on a deeply personal ethical level to individuals rather than making them society-wide policies. Global ethical policies will by necessity both run counter to the ethical opinion of many individuals, coercing citizens to act against their beliefs and hence violating their freedom and contain the temptation to adjust the policies to benefit the policymakers rather than the citizens" (Sandberg, 2001).

On a global scale, a transhumanist priority is considering the risks, uncertainties, and the magnitude of expected loss due to catastrophes. Existential Risk, as clarified by Nick Bostrom, considers three dimensions that describe the magnitude of risk, its scope, intensity, and probability. According to Bostrom, Founding Director of the Future of Humanity Institute, existential risk means: "[o]ne where an adverse outcome would either annihilate Earth-originating intelligent life or permanently and drastically curtail its potential" (2001).

"An existential risk is one where humankind is imperiled. Existential disasters have major adverse consequences for the course of human civilization for all time to come" (Bostrom, 2001).

SPECIALIZATION MODULES

- MIND: AGELESS THINKING
- BODY: HEALTH FITNESS
- SCIENCE & TECHNOLOGY
- CULTURAL ENGAGEMENT
- PROJECTS & PRODUCTS
- FINANCIAL SECURITY
- POLITICS & LEGISLATION

ADDITIONAL MODULES
Select 4 modules of your choice

- Stay Alive
- Stop Aging
- Nutrition
- Exercise
- Evidence-based
- Recent
- Transhumanism
- Events
- Education
- Resources
- Investments
- Independence
- RLX Rights
- Morphological Freedom

Be an Expert!
CERTIFICATE OF MERIT

- LIFE PROJECT DEVELOPER
- STAYING ALIVE STRATEGIST
- STOP AGING KNOWLEDGE LEADER
- RLX ENTREPRENEUR
- LONGLIFE MONEY MANAGER

CERTIFICATE OF MERIT

In recognition for observing the requirements
of one or more of the Learning Modules:

Life Project Developer
Staying Alive Strategist
Stop Aging Knowledge Leader
RLX Entrepreneur
LongLife Money Manager

September 22, 2018

CHAPTER 8

Is there transhumanist education?

Yes. There are numerous resources to learn about transhumanism. Nevertheless, there is a need for a field of study.

Education and its delivery model are changing. It is no longer the professor lecturing in front of an auditorium and student jotting down notes, awaiting acknowledgement. It has become fluid, interactive and a participatory, including production studio where students work in teams on projects and faculty mentors their learning experience. The format is synchronous and independent, with a continuous, iterative, and self-motivated pursuit of knowledge for both personal and professional goals. The model is anytime, anywhere, on-ground, one-one-one mentoring, online, virtual, videotaped lectures, and chat rooms with whiteboards and other collaborative tools.

Be informed and keep learning

The goals of a transhumanist educational platform for lifelong learning expands beyond academics and into the real-world experience, with hands-on participation within each course and related production studios where students work in teams.

The most sought out areas for continuous learning are in fields that are associated with job creation and cultural, economic, and political understanding. For example, ethics is an area where transhumanists need be informed about the pros and cons of emerging, exponential technologies and in what ways these technologies could alter the human condition. Knowing about the arguments stated by bioethicists and the general public is just part of the learning goal. Being able to debate arguments from an objective stance that addresses at all sides of an issue and sets forth a solid argument for the transhumanist perspective is the learning goal. Knowing the arguments and most effective terminology to use and reliable facts is crucial.

Another area for skill-building is in the realm of life extension sciences. To be able to identify evidence-based science from pseudo-science is crucial because at a time when the terms such as "stem cells" are marketing tools within the life extension industry, we need to be knowledgeable about what stems cells therapies are being used and how to identify questionable and potentially flawed stem-cell therapies from treatments that are medically acceptable.

The field of artificial intelligence is deeply rooted in transhumanist visions for the future. From research on perception and neuro networks to programming of AGI, why is the field crucial for humanity's future and how do we instill a positive relationship with supercomputers? Knowing the history of AI, its long winter, and resurgence toward the technological singularity is serious and science fact from science fiction understood within the technological sphere. AI is an area where people are deeply concerned and afraid. Knowing the challenges and the research and development within the field is clearly essential.

Likewise, the field of cybersecurity may seem daunting for someone outside network security, network engineering, or technology forensics, but we all need to understand the advances within of cybersecurity apply such advances to a future transhumanists trajectory of uploading and the need identify protection is a big issue when expanding personal identify across substrates.

Closer to the current timeframe and back to continuous learning in fields associated with job creation and cultural, economic, and political awareness, consider the issue that every day 10,000 baby boomers in the US turn 65 and will until approximately 2030. How are these people going to support themselves? Social security in the US is one way, but it may not be satisfying to not be part of the culture of entrepreneurs and innovators, educators and project leaders. Different countries have different statistics, but the fact is that people are living longer and may opt to continuing being a vital force in society—with a passion and purpose. Lifelong learning is an iterative process, we are never finished—we just keep getting smarter.

To prepare for lifelong learning, superlongevity is the future and indefinite lifespans are the goal. Developing curricula for tis goal requires certificates in key areas that will impact society. For the Radical Life Extension education (rlXedu) proposes certificates of merit, starting with five key professional fields. These field fill a gap in academic leaning curricula, within society as a general and advanced offering that meets the needs of generations who ae living longer, and also provides basic and advanced courses that are aligned with today's academic learning models. The five key fields are: Life Project Developer, Staying Alive Strategist, Stop Aging Knowledge Leader, Radical Life Extension Entrepreneur, and Superlongevity Money Manager. As an example, a Life Project Developer is an expert in project management and uses scrum, or other software, as a framework to take a project from a start point to a prototype. The skills of pitching the project or a venture capitalist and form a team are aligned with this skill set.

An area where the skills of a Life Project Developer, Superlongevity Money Manager, or rlX Entrepreneur are needed is within the political sphere, where the curricula offers Politics & Legislation as a means to learn about the current state of affairs within governance of people's rights to live longer and also the legislation concerning their future. Will people be taxes for living longer than a restricted lifespan?

The specific areas where the five professional fields integrate are as follows:

Unit 1: Healthy Mind - Ageless Thinking

Unit 2: Healthy Body - Ageless Body

> *Regenerative Generation*
>
> *Medical Science and Technology*
>
> *New Bodies*

Unit 3: Intelligence Growth & Critical Thinking

> *Exponential Lifelong Learning*
>
> *Assessing fact from fiction*
>
> *Identifying Primary Sources of Knowledge*

Unit 4: Financial Security

> *Be Prepared Financially*
>
> *Plan Financial Independence and Tax bracket*
>
> *Continue Earning Income*

Unit 5: Governance of Radical Life Extension

> *Get Involved with State Legislation*
>
> *Understand FDA Rules*
>
> *Join Political Initiatives*

SUGGESTED READING

Seminal ideas by leaders of their respective fields related to the transhumanist agenda and the growing movement.

The Transhumanist Reader:
Classical and Contemporary Essays on the Science, Technology, and Philosophy of the Human Future

APPENDIX

Scientific Research Organizations

Alcor Life Extension Foundation

Life Extension Foundation

Methuselah Foundation

SENS Research Foundation

The Brain Preservation Foundation

Twenty-First Century Medicine

Educational Research Organizations

Future of Humanity Institute

Healthy Life Extension Society

Humanity+

Institute for Ethics and Emerging Technologies

International Longevity Alliance

Life Extension Advocacy Foundation

Longevity Bridge

Maximum Life Foundation

Millennial Project

OpenCog Foundation | Building better minds together

RescueElders | Society for the Rescue of Our Elders

SingularityNET

World Future Society

H+ Members Organizations

Asociación Transhumanista Latinoamericana

Association Française Transhumaniste

Association Française Transhumaniste Technoprog

Christian Transhumanist Association

Humanity+, Inc.

London Futurists

Mormon Transhumanist Association

Network Transumanisti Italiani

Political Groups

Parti Transhumaniste France

Science Party

Technoprogressive

Transhuman National Committee

Transhuman Party

Transhumanist Party

Transhumanist Party Global

Transpolitica

Suggested H+ Resources

H+ Influential Leaders: humanityplus.org/leaders.org

H+Pedia: hpluspedia.org/wiki/Main_Page

h+ Magazine: hplusmagazine.com

Futurism: futurism.com

Suggested H+ books

1312 Paradiso, Divine Comedy, Inferno (1320) | Dante Alighieri

1957 New Bottles for New Wine | Julian Huxley

1959 The Future of Man | Teilhard de Chardin

1962 The Prospect of Immortality | Robert C.W. Ettinger

1972 Man into Superman: The Startling Potential of Human Evolution And How To Be Part of It | Robert Ettinger

1973 Up-Wingers: A Futurist Manifesto | F. M. Esfandiary

1987 Engines of Creation: The Coming Era of Nanotechnology | K. Eric Drexler

1989 Are You a Transhuman? Monitoring and Stimulating Your Personal Rate of Growth in a Rapidly Changing World | FM Esfandiary (aka 2030)

1990 Mind Children: The Future of Robot and Human Intelligence | Hans Moravec

1991 Great Mambo Chicken & The Transhuman Condition | Ed Regis

1995 The Hedonistic Imperative | David Pearce

1999 The Mitochondrial Free Radical Theory of Aging | Aubrey De Grey

2001 The Age of Spiritual Machines: When Computers Exceed Human Intelligence | Raymond Kurzweil

2002 Our Posthuman Future: Consequences of the Biotechnology Revolution | Francis Fukuyama

2002 Redesigning Humans: Choosing our genes, changing our future | Gregory Stock

2004 Citizen Cyborg: Why Democratic Societies Must Respond To The Redesigned Human Of The Future | James Hughes

2005 Designer Evolution: A Transhumanist Manifesto |
Simon S. Young

2005 Fantastic Voyage: Live Long Enough to Live Forever |
Raymond Kurzweil

2005 Radical Evolution: The Promise and Peril of Enhancing
Our Minds, Our Bodies and What It Means to Be Human |
Joel Garreau

2006 The End of History and the Last Man | Francis Fukuyama

2006 The Singularity Is Near: When Humans Transcend Biology
| Raymond Kurzweil

2007 Ending Aging: The Rejuvenation Breakthroughs That
Could Reverse Human Aging in Our Lifetime | Aubrey De Grey

2007 The Emotion Machine | Marvin Minsky

2009 Nanotechnology and Society | Fritz Allhoff, Patrick Lin

2009 Transcend: Nine Steps to Living Well Forever |
Ray Kurzweil; Terry Grossman

2011 Humanity 2.0: What It Means to Be Human Past, Present
and Future | Steve Fuller

2011 Transhumanism and Its Critics | (numerous authors)

2012 How to Create a Mind: The Secret of Human Thought
Revealed | Raymond Kurzweil

2013 Humanity Enhanced: Genetic Choice and the Challenge
for Liberal Democracies | Russell Blackford

2013 Radical Abundance: How a Revolution in Nanotechnology
Will Change Civilization | K. Eric Drexler

2013 The Transhumanist Reader: Classical and Contemporary
Essays on the Science, Technology, and Philosophy of the
Human Future | Max More & Natasha Vita-More

2013 The Transhumanist Wager | Zoltan Istvan

2014 A History of Life-Extensionism in the Twentieth Century | Ilia Stambler

2014 Abundance: The Future is Better Than You Think | Peter H. Diamandis, Steven Kotler

2014 Intelligence Unbound: The Future of Uploaded and Machine Minds | Russell Blackford & Damien Broderick

2014 Regenesis: How Synthetic Biology Will Reinvent Nature and Ourselves | Ed Regis, George Church

2014 Superintelligence: Paths, Dangers, Strategies | Nick Bostrom

2015 A Dangerous Master: How to Keep Technology from Slipping Beyond Our Control | Wendell Wallach

2015 Aging: The Longevity Dividend | S. Jay Olshansky

2015 Exponential Organizations | Salim Ismail

2015 Surviving AI: The promise and peril of artificial intelligence | Calum Chace

2015 Tesla, SpaceX, and the Quest for a Fantastic Future | Elon Musk

2016 Advancing Conversations: Advocate For An Indefinite Human Lifespan | D. Lain & Aubrey de Grey

2016 AGI Revolution: An Inside View of the Rise of Artificial General Intelligence | Ben Goertzel

2016 Cracking the Aging Code | Josh Mitteldorf & Dorion Sagan

2016 Machine Ethics and Robot Ethics | Wendell Wallach

2016 Technoprog (Présence/Essai) | Didier Coeurnelle

2016 The Abolition of Aging: The forthcoming radical extension of healthy human longevity | David Wood

2016 The Economic Singularity: Artificial intelligence and the death of capitalism | Calum Chace

2016 The Ethics of Human Enhancement: Understanding the Debate | Steve Clarke & Julian Savulescu

2017 Abundance | Peter H. Diamandis

2017 Can Biotechnology Abolish Suffering? | David Pearce & Magnus Vinding

2017 Juvenescence: Investing in the age of longevity | Jim Mellon & Al Chalabi

2017 Science Fiction and the Moral Imagination: Visions, Minds, Ethics | Russell Blackford

2018 Artificial Intelligence and the Two Singularities | Calum Chace

2018 La muerte de la muerte: La posibilidad científica de la inmortalidad física y su defensa moral | José Luis Cordeiro & David Wood

2018 Singolarità - David Orban

2019 Danielle: Chronicles of a Superheroine l Ray Kurzweil

Notes

[1] Keynotes included Ronald Bailey, Science Correspondent, Reason Magazine; Aubrey de Grey, University of Cambridge, Department of Genetics; Robert A. Freitas author of Nanomedicine; Raymond Kurzweil, Kurzweil Technologies; author of The Age of Spiritual Machines; Max More, Philosophical Strategist and author of "Elements of a New Enlightenment"; Marvin Minsky, MIT and Author, Society of Mind; Christine Peterson, President Foresight Institute and author of Leaping the Abyss: Putting Group Genius to Work; Michael D. Shapiro, University of Southern California Law School; Lee Silver, Professor at Princeton University in the Department of Molecular Biology; Gregory Stock, Director, Program on Medicine, Technology, and Society UCLA's School of Public Health; Natasha Vita-More, former President, Extropy Institute and innovator of "Primo Posthuman"; Roy L. Walford, Professor of Pathology at the UCLA School of Medicine and author of Maximum Life Span; and Michael West, President and CEO, Advanced Cell Technology

RESOLVE TO EVOLVE

Join Humanity+, Inc.

References

Figure 1. Humanity+ logo.

Figure 2. Vita-More, N. (May 26, 2017). "Technology of Human Enhancement: The Scope of a Regenerative Generation." Lagos, Nigeria.

Alberts, B., Johnson, A., Lewis, J., et al. (2002). "Cancer" in Molecular Biology of Cell. 4th Ed. New York: Garland Science, p. 1014.

Alighieri, Dante. (1312). *Paradiso of the Divina Commedia.* (n.p.)

Bailey, R. (February 9, 2007). "On Human Dignity". *Reason.* Available: https://reason.com/archives/2007/02/09/on-human-dignity

Bernstein, J. (December 14, 1981) "A.I." in *The New Yorker.* Available: https://www.newyorker.com/magazine/1981/12/14/a-i

Bostrom, N. 2002. "Existential Risks: Analyzing Human Extinction Scenarios and Related Hazards". Journal of Evolution and Technology, Vol. 9, No. 1. [First version: 2001)]

Bostrom, N. (2013). "Existential Risks FAQ". Version 1.2. Available http://www.existential-risk.org/faq.pdf

Courau, L. (1996). "Natasha Vita-More <<Transhuman Manifesto>>. *La Spirale.* Available: https://laspirale.org/texte-33-natasha-vita-more-transhuman-manifesto.html

Diamandis, P., Kotler, S. (2014). *Abundance: The Future Is Better Than You Think.* Free Press, Tantor Media. (pp. p. 6, 7, 11).

Drexler, E.K. (1986). *Engines of Creation: The Coming Era of Nanotechnology.* Anchor, p. 3, 239.

Elliot, T.S. (1964). "The Cocktail Party". Mariner Books.

El Issa, E. (2017). "2017 American Household Credit Card Debt Study". Nerdwallet. Available: https://www.nerdwallet.com/blog/average-credit-card-debt-household/

Esfandiary, FM. (1978). *Optimism One*. New York: Popular Library.

Esfandiary, FM. (1977). *Upwingers a Futurist Manifesto*. John Day, pp. 21-25.

Ettinger, C.W. (1964). *The Prospect of Immortality*. (n.p.).

Ettinger, C.W. (1972). *Man into Superman*. (n.p.)

Extropy: The Journal of Transhumanist Thought. (1988). Vol. 1. Extropy Institute.

Fessenden, M. (January 22, 2016). "There Are Now More Americans Over Age 100 and They're Living Longer Than Ever". SmartNews. Available: https://www.smithsonianmag.com/smart-news/there-are-more-americans-over-age-100-now-and-they-are-living-longer-180957914/

Forbes. (Sep 12, 2016). "What Will Humans Look Like 100,000 Years From Now?" Available: https://www.forbes.com/sites/quora/2016/09/12/what-will-humans-look-like-100000-years-from-now/#129449a01403

Future of Life Institute. "An Open Letter". Available: https://futureoflife.org/ai-open-letter/

Goertzel, B. (2012). "Future Day: March 1, 2012". Humanity+ Press. Available: http://hplusmagazine.com/2012/02/10/future-day-march-1-2012/

Goertzel, B. (2016). *AGI Revolution: An Inside View of the Rise of Artificial General Intelligence*. Los Angeles: Humanity+ Press.

Goertzel, B. and Pennachin, C. (2007) *Artificial General Intelligence*. Springer. Available: https://link.springer.com/book/10.1007/978-3-540-68677-4#toc

Haraway, D. (1991). "Cyborg Manifesto: Science, Technology, and Socialist-Feminism in the Late Twentieth Century". *Simians, Cyborgs and Women: The Reinvention of Nature.* New York: Routledge.

Institute for Ethics and Emerging Technologies. (n.a.) "precautionary vs. Proactionary principles. Available: https://ieet.org/index.php/tpwiki/Precautionary_vs._proactionary_principles

Kurzweil, R. (2006). The Singularity is Near: When Humans Transcend Biology. Penguin Books, p. 7.

Langdon, A., Crook, N., and Dantas, G. (13 April 2016). "The effects of antibiotics on the microbiome throughout development and alternative approaches for therapeutic modulation. In Genome Medicine" Available: https://genomemedicine.biomedcentral.com/articles/10.1186/s13073-016-0294-z

Leary, T. (1989). "Exo-Psychology". Valle R.S., von Eckartsberg R. (eds) *Metaphors of Consciousness.* Boston: Springer, pp. 179-197.

Margulis, L., Sagan, D. (2000), What is Life? Berkeley and Los Angeles: University of California Press, p. 215.

Mattmiller, B. (December 10, 2007). "Genome study places modern humans in the evolutionary fast lane". University of Wisconsin-Madison News. Available: https://news.wisc.edu/genome-study-places-modern-humans-in-the-evolutionary-fast-lane/

McAuliffe, K. (Feb. 9, 2009). "They Don't Make Homo Sapiens Like They Used To". *Discover.* Available: http://discovermagazine.com/2009/mar/09-they-dont-make-homo-sapiens-like-they-used-to

McKechnie, J. (1983). *Webster's New Universal Unabridged Dictionary*. London: Dorset.

More, M. (1993). "Morphological Freedom". (n.w.)

More, M. (2004). "Superlongevity without Overpopulation", chapter in *The Scientific Conquest of Death*. Immortality Institute. http://www.amazon.com/exec/obidos/ASIN/9875611352/qid=1124056251/sr=2-1/ref=pd_bbs_b_2_1/002-3345332-4734455

More, M. (2013). "Proactionary Principle". More, M., Vita-More, N. (eds) *The Transhumanist Reader: Classical and Contemporary Essays on the Science, Technology, and Philosophy of the Future Human*. Wiley Blackwell.

Olshansky, J., Carnes, B.A. (2003). *The Quest for Immortality: Science at the Frontiers of Aging*. WW. Norton.

Pearson, D., Shaw, S. (1983). *Life Extension: A Practical Scientific Approach*. Grant Central Pub.

Research Priorities for Robust and Beneficial Artificial Intelligence: an Open Letter". Future of Life Institute. Available: https://futureoflife.org/ai-open-letter

Sandberg, A. (2001). "Morphological Freedom – Why We not just Want it, but *Need* it". Available: http://www.aleph.se/Nada/Texts/MorphologicalFreedom.htm

Sandberg, A. and Bostrom, N. (2008). "Whole Brain Emulation A Roadmap. Technical Report #2008-3", Future of Humanity Institute, Oxford University. Available: http://www.fhi.ox.ac.uk/brain-emulation-roadmap-report.pdf

Schultz, C. (November 29, 2012). "Humans Have Been Evolving Like Crazy Over the Past Few Thousand Years". *Smithsonian Smart News*. Available: http://www.smithsonianmag.com/smart-news/humans-have-been-evolving-like-crazy-over-the-past-few-thousand-years-147494375/

Smithsonian National Museum of Natural History. (n.d.). "What does it mean to be human?". Available: http://humanorigins. si.edu/education/introduction-human-evolution

Stock, J.T. ((2008 Jul; 9(Suppl 1): S51-S54. Doi: 10.1038/ embor200863. Science and Society. EMBO Reports. Available: https://www.ncbi.nlm.nih.gov/pmc/articles/ PMC3327538/

Technoprogressive Declaration. Available: https://transvision-conference.org/tpdec2017/

Teilhard, P. (De Chardin). (1959). *The Future of Man*. Editions de Seuil.

The Reader's Digest Condensed Books. Vol. 3. (1996). Reader's Digest Assoc.

Tripp, M. (1974). "Transhumans – 2000". *Woman in the Year 2000*. Arbor House, pp. 291-298.

Vinge, V. (1993). "The Coming Technological Singularity: How to Survive in the Post-Human Era". Vision-21 Interdisciplinary Science and Engineering in the Era of Cyberspace. NASA Conference Publication 10129, pp. 11-22.

Vita-More, N. (2010). "Transhumanism: The Way of the Future". *The Scavenger*. Available: http://www.thescavenger. net/media-a-technology-sp-9915/media-a-technology/175-transhumanism-the-way-of-the-future-98432.html

Vita-More, N. and McMahon, K. (2013). Body by Design. Available https://www.youtube.com/ watch?v=vVG2MbpHd4o

Vita-More, N. (2006). "Primo Posthuman". *The Singularity is Near: When Humans Transcend Biology*. Penguin Books, p. 583.

Walford, R. (1985). *Maximum Life Span*. W.W. Norton.

ABOUT THE AUTHOR

Natasha Vita-More PhD

"If you want to meet a potential early adopter of these revolutionary changes, look no further than Natasha Vita-More."
Wired 2000

Professor Vita-More holds a PhD, University of Plymouth, School of Media Arts, Design and Architecture; a MPhil, University of Plymouth, School of Communications and Media Studies; an MSc, University of Houston, School of Sciences and Technology - Future Studies; a BFA, University of Memphis, School of Fine Arts. She was filmmaker-in-residence, University of Colorado; and holds Certificates as Paralegal, Nutrition and Sports Training, American Muscle & Fitness Association.

Called an "early adapter of revolutionary changes" (*Wired* magazine, 2000) and a "role model for superlongevity" (Village Voice, 2001), her conceptual whole-body prototype received international recognition. While her media design works have been honored at Women in Video, the Moscow Film Festival, her most recent scientific research has been a breakthrough within the field of cryonics and long-term memory of the simple animal, the *C. elegans*.

Website: www.natashavita-more.com

Made in the USA
Coppell, TX
24 October 2020